Key Stage 1 Reading

Revision and Practice Questions

Helen Betts

RISING STARS

Acknowledgements

Rising Stars would like to thank the following trial schools for their feedback on the Achieve Key Stage 1 series: Edgewood Primary School, Notts, Henwick Primary School, London, Tennyson Road Primary, Beds, Christ Church Church of England (VC) Primary School, Wiltshire, Churchfields, The Village School, Wiltshire and Chacewater Community Primary School, Cornwall.

The Publishers would like to thank the following for permission to reproduce copyright material.

Photo credits: page 10 © tirc83/iStockphoto; page 22 © juefraphoto/Shutterstock; page 40 © aldra/iStockphoto; page 42 © wilsondmir/iStockphoto; page 56 © Mr. SUTTIPON YAKHAM/Shutterstock.

Page 8 *Tonight is the Sleepover* by Geoff Patton. Permission is granted to reproduce extracts from 'Tonight is the Sleepover' by Laguna Bay Publishing; Page 10 *Rabbit (My New Pet Series)* by Jinny Johnson. Appleseed Editions Ltd; Page 12 Extract from *Robovac* by Susan Gates, ORT Treetops (OUP, 2006), copyright © Liz Miles 2006, reprinted by permission of Oxford University Press; Page 16 Extract from *The Magic Paintbrush* by Liz Miles, ORT Traditional Tales (OUP, 2011), copyright © Liz Miles 2011, reprinted by permission of Oxford University Press; Page 24 from George and the Dragon by Anne Adeney, first published in the UK by Franklin Watts, an imprint of Hachette Children's Books, Carmelite House, 50 Victoria Embankment, London, EC4Y 0DZ; Page 26 *The Giant Squid*. © The Trustees of the Natural History Museum, London; Page 28 *Daddy Fell into the Pond* by Alfred Noyes. The Society of Authors as the Literary Representative of the Estate of Alfred Noyes; Page 30 *Plop the Owl* from *The Owl Who Was Afraid of the Dark* by Jill Tomlinson. Text copyright © 1968 The Estate of Jill Tomlinson. Published by Egmont UK and used with kind permission; Page 34 *Eating food.* Reproduced from *Look Inside Your Body* by permission of Usborne Publishing, 83–85 Saffron Hill, London EC1N 8RT, UK. www.usborne.com. Copyright © 2011; Page 38 *Broad Bean Snack* from *Grow Your Own Snack* by John Malam. Reprinted by permission of Raintree. Page 40 from *Dealing with Feeling Happy* by Isabel Thomas. © 2013 by Capstone. All rights reserved; Page 42 from *The Usborne Children's Picture Atlas* by Linda Edwards. Reproduced from *Children's Picture Atlas* by permission of Usborne Publishing, 83–85 Saffron Hill, London EC1N 8RT, UK. www.usborne.com. Copyright © 2003; Page 44 from *See Inside Space* by Katie Daynes. Reproduced from *See Inside Space* by permission of Usborne Publishing, 83–85 Saffron Hill, London EC1N 8RT, UK. www.usborne.com. Copyright © 2008 Usborne; Page 46 from *George Saves the World by Lunchtime* by Jo Readman. Published by Eden Children's Books. Reproduced by permission of The Random House Group Ltd; Page 52 *Space Poem* from *I'm a Little Alien* by James Carter published by Frances Lincoln Ltd, copyright © 2014. Reproduced by permission of Frances Lincoln Ltd; Page 54 Extract from *Mr Crookodile* by John Bush. Text copyright © 2006 John Bush. Published by Egmont UK Ltd and used with permission. Page 56 Adapted from Article from Tiggywinkles, Wildlife Hospital Trust, Registered Charity Number 286447; Page 58 From *Cliffhanger* by Jacqueline Wilson, published by Corgi Children's. Reproduced by permission of The Random House Group Ltd; Page 60 *Oggy* from *I'm a Little Alien* by James Carter published by Frances Lincoln Ltd, copyright © 2014. Reproduced by permission of Frances Lincoln Ltd.

Every effort has been made to trace all copyright holders, but if any have been inadvertently overlooked, the Publishers will be pleased to make the necessary arrangements at the first opportunity.

Although every effort has been made to ensure that website addresses are correct at time of going to press, Rising Stars cannot be held responsible for the content of any website mentioned in this book. It is sometimes possible to find a relocated web page by typing in the address of the home page for a website in the URL window of your browser.

Hachette UK's policy is to use papers that are natural, renewable and recyclable products and made from wood grown in sustainable forests. The logging and manufacturing processes are expected to conform to the environmental regulations of the country of origin.

ISBN: 978-1-78339-536-1

© Hodder & Stoughton Limited

Reprinted 2016 (twice), 2018 (twice), 2019

First published in 2015 by Hodder & Stoughton Limited (for its Rising Stars imprint, part of the Hodder Education Group)
An Hachette UK Company
Carmelite House
50 Victoria Embankment
London EC4Y 0DZ

www.risingstars-uk.com

The right of Helen Betts to be identified as the author of this work had been asserted by her in accordance with the Copyright, Design and Patents Act 1998.

Author: Helen Betts
Series Editor: Siobhan Skeffington
Accessibility reviewer: Vivien Kilburn
Publishers: Kate Jamieson and Laura White
Project Manager: Vanessa Handscombe
Editorial: Sarah Davies, Elizabeth Evans and Faye Cheeseman
Illustrations: Adam Linley/Beehive Illustration and Judy Brown/Beehive Illustration

Cover design: Burville-Riley Partnership
Text design and typeset by Out of House Publishing
Printed in Slovenia

A catalogue record for this title is available from the British Library.

Contents

Introduction 4

How to use this book 6

Using clues 8

What happens next? 16

Understanding word meanings 22

The order of events 32

Finding information 38

Character and events 46

Explaining what you have read 54

Glossary 62

Answers 63

Introduction

Hello, I'm Seren. Welcome to the Achieve Reading Revision and Practice Book.

I'll be your guide as you work through the book. I'll tell you about each topic and what you need to know. Together, we'll revise all the Reading topics that you learned in Years 1 and 2.

We'll also practise some questions for each topic. The 'Team Achieve' will show you how to answer the questions.

Let's meet the team.

Hi, I'm Rhys.

Hello, I'm Leena.

Hello,
I'm Kofi.

Hi,
I'm Zofia.

Let's go.

5

How to use this book

In this section Seren tells you what you will need to know for each section for the end of Key Stage 1 National Tests. Words in **bold** can be found in the Glossary on page 62.

SEQUENCING

The order of events

You need to show that you understand the **sequence** of **events**. This means explaining in what order things happen in different **texts** (pieces of writing).

You need to read this piece of writing carefully to answer the questions that follow.

Read this

Making Pancakes

We got out a big dish and I climbed on a stool and reached the flour down from the cupboard, knocking over the sugar as I did it. That was the first accident. You know what sugar's like – it seems to get all over the place – in the bread and butter, all over the floor, and some of it was on Ruthie's head. She didn't mind. She was licking it up as it trickled down her face. We put some of the flour in the dish and scraped the sugar into it off the table.

From *Making Pancakes When My Mother Was Out* by Paddy Kinsale

These tips give you good ideas on how to answer the questions, or useful information on the topic.

Top tips

- When you are asked to *Number the sentences,* write a different number in each box.
- Check your answer to see if the sentences are in the correct order.

This question lets you practise the skills for the topic. It is just like a real test question so gives you practice for the end of Key Stage 1 National Tests.

The flow chart shows you how to answer the Let's try question. You can learn the method and use it to answer similar questions in this book and in the National Tests.

Identify and explain the sequence of events in texts

Let's try

Number the sentences from **1** to **4** to show the order in which they happened. Number **1** has been done for you.

- [ ] The sugar was knocked over.
- [ ] They put some flour in the dish.
- [1] The children got out a dish.
- [ ] Ruthie licked up some of the sugar.

1 Read the question and read it again. What do you have to do?

I need to put the sentences in the right order.

2 What should you do first?

Read the story again. Find each event that is in the question.

3 Number 1 is done for you. Decide which sentence will be number 2. Then move on to number 3 and number 4. Check your answer.

The sentences should be numbered 2, 4, 1, 3.

Your turn

1 What was the **last** thing the children did? [1 mark]

Tick **one**.

They put the sugar into the dish. [ ]
They got the flour from the cupboard. [ ]
They put sugar in Ruthie's hair. [ ]
They put the flour on the table. [ ]

In this section you will find practice questions for you to answer. Try to use the method from the flow chart or the Top tips to help you.

Using clues

You need to work out things that the writer has not told you. To do this you can use clues in the **text** (a piece of writing). Clues might come from something a **character** says or does, or something that happens.

Read this

The sleepover

It's tonight! Sam is coming for a sleepover.
I can't wait.
Mum can! She says that *this* time we have to do the sleep part of the sleepover.
I say, "Mum, the best part of a sleepover is the staying awake all night part."
Mum says maybe there will be no sleepover after all.
I say, "I'm only joking." But I have my fingers crossed behind my back. It's hard to go to sleep when you are having a sleepover.

From *Tonight is the Sleepover* by Geoff Patton

Top tip

Read all the choices in the list, even if you think you have found the correct answer.

Let's try

Mum says that this time the children *have to do the sleep part of the sleepover*.
What does this tell you?

Tick **one**.

Mum doesn't mind if they stay awake all night. ☐

Last time they had a sleepover they didn't sleep. ☐

The children have never had a sleepover before. ☐

The boy is excited about having a sleepover. ☐

1 Read the question and read it again. What do you have to do?

I need to decide what it shows when Mum says they have to sleep this time.

2 What might this mean?

Last time they didn't sleep much.

3 Read all the answer choices. Which one fits what you have found? Check your answer.

Last time they had a sleepover they didn't sleep. ✓

Your turn

1 Why does the boy find it hard to go to sleep at a sleepover? [1 mark]

Tick **one**.

He is too excited to sleep. ☐

He doesn't like sleeping. ☐

He is too worried to sleep. ☐

He always finds sleeping hard. ☐

Read this

Pet rabbit

A rabbit has a plump, rounded body, long ears and big eyes. Rabbits are **good-tempered** and make great family pets. They are easily scared, so we must treat them very gently. Pet rabbits like company and usually live for between seven and ten years.

A rabbit's coat should be smooth and shiny, with no bare patches.

From *Rabbit* (*My New Pet* series) by Jinny Johnson

Glossary

good-tempered   friendly, calm

Top tips

- If you are asked to **find** and **copy**, check whether you need to copy a *word*, a *group of words* or a *sentence*.
- Don't add in extra words. It might help to underline the word or words first.

Let's try

Why might you decide to get more than one pet rabbit?

_____

1 Read the question and read it again. What do you have to do?

I need to say why you might get more than one pet rabbit.

2 Does the text give you the answer?

No. It doesn't say anything about the number of rabbits. I will have to work it out.

3 Can you see any clues?

Yes. It says that *rabbits like company*. This might be a reason to get more than one.

4 Write your answer. Check your answer.

Because rabbits like company.

Your turn

1 **Find** and **copy one** group of words that shows **why** it is a good idea to be careful and quiet around rabbits. [1 mark]

_____

Read this

Robo-Vac

Suddenly, Connor had a brilliant idea.
He took Robo-Vac to his sister Gemma's bedroom.
Gemma was as tidy as Connor was messy. Nothing
in her bedroom was ever out of place. She would get
on with Robo-Vac really well.
"Hey, Gemma," said Connor.
"Do you want your own cleaning robot?"
"Wow!" said Gemma. "A cleaning robot.
What a great idea."
Connor went back to his own bedroom.
At last he'd got rid of Robo-Vac.
He threw a few things on the floor.
Now he could be as messy as
he liked …

From *Robo-Vac* by Susan Gates

Top tip

Check if you need to write just one word or give an explanation.

Let's try

Why does Connor think that Gemma will like Robo-Vac?

_____

1 | Read the question and read it again. What do you have to do? | I need to say why Connor thinks Gemma will like Robo-Vac.

2 | What do you know about Gemma? What do you know about Robo-Vac? | Gemma is very neat and tidy. Robo-Vac is a cleaning robot.

3 | Does this answer the question? | Yes. Gemma will like Robo-Vac because she doesn't like mess.

4 | Check your answer.

Your turn

1 How did Gemma feel when Connor told her about Robo-Vac?
Tick **one**. [1 mark]

relieved ☐   excited ☐

annoyed ☐   clever ☐

2 At the end, what did Connor do that showed he was happy to be rid of Robo-Vac? [1 mark]

_____

Read this

The Snowman

Once there was a snowman
Stood outside the door,
Thought he'd like to come inside
And run around the floor;
Thought he'd like to warm himself
By the **firelight** red;
Thought he'd like to clamber up
On that big white bed.

So he called the North Wind, "Help me now I pray.
I'm completely frozen, standing here all day."
So the North Wind came along and blew him in the door –
And now there's nothing left of him
But a puddle on the floor.

By Anonymous

Glossary
firelight   light from a fire in
             a fireplace

Top tips

- Read the poem at least twice.
- Check if you need to write just one word or give an explanation.

Let's try

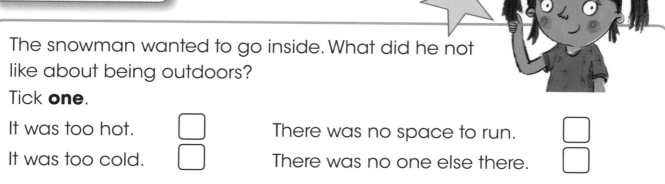

The snowman wanted to go inside. What did he not like about being outdoors?

Tick **one**.

It was too hot. ☐   There was no space to run. ☐

It was too cold. ☐   There was no one else there. ☐

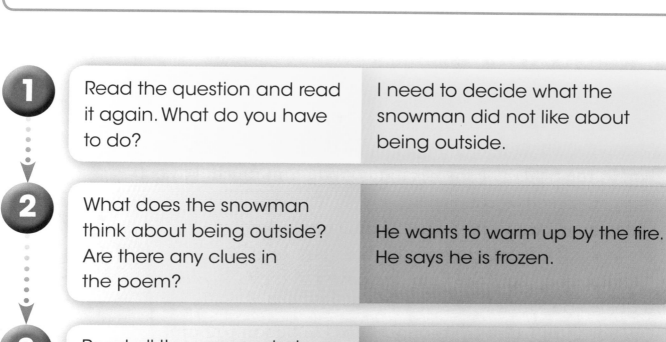

1 Read the question and read it again. What do you have to do?

I need to decide what the snowman did not like about being outside.

2 What does the snowman think about being outside? Are there any clues in the poem?

He wants to warm up by the fire. He says he is frozen.

3 Read all the answer choices. Which one best fits with these clues? Check your answer.

It was too cold.

Your turn

1 Look at the last two lines of the poem. Explain **what** has happened to the snowman and **why**.   [2 marks]

_____

_____

What happens next?

You need to **predict** (say) what might happen next in a story or other **text** (piece of writing). This means using what you have read to say what a **character** might say or do next, or what might happen to them.

Read this

The Magic Paintbrush

Every day, Ho looked after a rich farmer's cattle. He took hay to the field. The farmer did not pay him much. Ho had only dry bread to eat.

One day a very thin, old man came up the lane. He looked hungry. Ho gave his bread to the man.

"Thank you," said the man. He gave Ho a gift. It was a golden paintbrush.

"What shall I paint?" thought Ho. He began to paint some hay. The hay became real! "This is a magic paintbrush!" said Ho.

The sun was hot. The stream was dry. So Ho painted a blue stream. The stream became real! Now the people and the animals had water to drink.

The rich farmer had lots of food to eat. But the children and workers were hungry.

From *The Magic Paintbrush* by Liz Miles

Top tip

Think about all you have read to help you predict more of the story.

Let's try

How do you think the people felt towards Ho after he painted the stream?

Tick **one**.

angry because he didn't pay them much ☐

grateful because they had water to drink now ☐

cross because the stream was so dry ☐

happy because he gave hay to their animals ☐

1 Read the question and read it again. What do you have to do? | I need to decide how the people felt towards Ho after he painted the stream.

2 What do you know from the story about the stream that Ho painted? | The stream became real.

3 How might the people have felt about Ho? Why? | Pleased because they had water to drink now.

4 Read all the answer choices. Which one fits best with what you know? Check your answer. | grateful because they had water to drink now ☑

Your turn

1 What do you think Ho might do next? [1 mark]

_____

Read this

Jack and the Beans

"Look what I've got for you!" Jack's uncle said to him, rattling a jar.

"What is it?" frowned Jack.

"Jumping beans!" smiled his uncle. "They are from **South America**!"

"Do they really jump?" asked Jack.

"Of course they do," replied his uncle. To show Jack, he put a few beans on the coffee table. They started jumping like mad.

Then one day Grandma came to stay. She knew nothing about the jumping beans. So when she found them in the kitchen one morning she cooked them for Jack's breakfast. Jack was in a hurry to go to school that day. He did not realise what they were until he had gobbled up the lot!

From *Jumping Jack* by A. H. Benjamin

Glossary
South America   a very large area of land made up of many countries

Top tip

Read all the choices in the list, even if you think you have found the correct answer.

Let's try

What might happen next to Jack?

_____

1 Read the question and read it again. What do you have to do? | I need to say what might happen next to Jack.

2 What do you know from the story so far? | Jack has some jumping beans. He has eaten all of them.

3 What might happen to Jack now? | He might start to jump about.

4 Check your answer.

Your turn

1 What do you think Grandma might say when she finds out what has happened?

[1 mark]

Tick **one**.

"I know all about jumping beans!" ☐

"I thought they were ordinary beans!" ☐

"Jumping beans are good for you!" ☐

"Eat your breakfast up, Jack!" ☐

Read this

Kitty and the Babysitter

Kitty heard Mum talking quietly to the babysitter in the hall, and just managed to catch the words, "... safely in bed."
She frowned. "But I don't want to go to bed," she muttered to herself. "And I jolly well won't. I'll hide – right now!" She jumped out of bed, ran into the spare room and crouched down behind the bed.
"When the silly old babysitter goes into my room to check me and say goodnight, she'll get a surprise," Kitty thought. And she settled down to wait for the fuss.

Christine the babysitter came upstairs, tiptoed past Kitty's room, and went to make sure Daniel was putting himself to bed. She was glad Kitty's room was so quiet. She did not look in. She went downstairs again, and turned on the television.
Kitty waited to be found. She waited and waited.

From *I Don't Want To!* by Bel Mooney

Top tip

When you are asked to say what might happen, there is sometimes more than one correct answer.

Let's try

Think about all you have read.
What do you think is most likely to happen next and **why**?

_____

_____

1 Read the question and read it again. What do you have to do?

I need to say what might happen next, and why. I will need to explain my answer.

2 What do you know from the story so far?

Kitty hid in the spare room. The babysitter went upstairs but did not check Kitty's room. Kitty is waiting to be found. It says _She waited and waited._

3 What might happen next?

Kitty might come out of her hiding place. Or she might fall asleep. Or the babysitter might find her in the end.

4 Choose one of your ideas. You must explain why you think this. Check your answer.

Kitty might fall asleep because she's been waiting for a long time.

Your turn

 1 What do you think Mum might have said to Kitty the next day?

[1 mark]

_____

Understanding word meanings

A word can have different meanings in different **texts** (pieces of writing). You need to show that you understand the meanings of words (e.g. *enormous*) and **phrases** (e.g. *the enormous monster*).

Read this

Mole
velvet coat
sharp teeth
spade hand
digs beneath

soil sprays
black fountains
high hills
small mountains

pink snout
seeks worms
bites wriggles
eats squirms

By Jan Dean

Glossary
velvet   a soft, furry material

Top tips

- If you are asked to **find** and **copy**, check whether you need to copy a *word*, a *group of words* or a *sentence*.
- Think about what your chosen word, or words, should mean.
- Remember to copy the text exactly. Underline the words to help you.

Let's try

Look at the **last verse**.
Find and **copy one** word which shows that the mole is trying to find something.

_____

1 | Read the question and read it again. What do you have to do? | I need to find and copy one word in the last verse that shows the mole is trying to find something.

2 | Read the last verse carefully. Do any of the words mean the same as or nearly the same as *find*? | If you *seek* something, you are trying to find it.

3 | Copy this word onto the answer line. Do not write any other words. | I need to write the word *seeks*.

4 | Check your answer. |

Your turn

1 Look at this line from the poem: *bites wriggles*
Find and **copy** another word that means the same as *wriggles.*

[1 mark]

_____

Read this

George and the Dragon

The foulest **odour** that George had ever smelt filled the air. But the dragon was nowhere to be seen. Suddenly there was a boom like angry thunder. The gigantic dragon **soared** down upon him from the sky. Its vast green wings blocked out the sun but George could still see the many rows of sharp teeth that glistened in the creature's open mouth.

From *George and the Dragon* by Anne Adeney

Glossary

odour   smell
soared   flew

Top tips

- Think: what do your chosen words need to show?
- Don't underline more words than you are asked for.

Let's try

Underline a **group** of **two** words that shows the dragon smelt horrible.

1 Read the question and read it again. What do you have to do?

I need to find and underline a group of two words that shows the dragon smelt horrible.

2 Can you find any words meaning *smell* and *horrible*?

The glossary says that *odour* is another word for *smell*. *Foulest* means it wasn't nice.

3 Underline these words. Don't underline more than two words.

I need to underline the words *foulest odour* in the text.

4 Check your answer.

Your turn

Its vast green wings blocked out the sun …
What does the word *vast* mean in this sentence?   [1 mark]

_____

Read this

The Giant Squid

Not many creatures dare to face the giant squid. The courageous **sperm whale** seems to have no fear of the squid, but the whales don't always come away unharmed. Many have nasty **sucker scars** and we can only imagine the underwater battles between these two remarkable creatures.

Not many people have ever seen a giant squid alive. Most are either found dead on beaches or in the stomachs of sperm whales. However, one fisherman caught a giant squid in his net. This giant squid is very important as it was not only alive but also complete.

Adapted from The Natural History Museum website

Glossary

sperm whale	a type of whale that feeds on squid
sucker scars	marks left by the suckers on the squid's tentacles

Top tip

If you are asked to *Draw a line to match,* only draw one line to each choice.

Let's try

Draw a line to match each word with its meaning in the text.

courageous •   • amazing

unharmed •   • brave

remarkable •   • not hurt

1   Read the question and read it again. What do you have to do? | I need to match each word with its meaning.

2   Find each of the words in the text. Do you know what any of them mean? | I know that *unharmed* means *not hurt*, and *courageous* means *brave*.

3   What about *remarkable*? The word left in the question is *amazing*. Would this fit in the text? | Yes. The text says they are *remarkable creatures*.

4   Now draw lines to match each word with one meaning. Check your answer. | I need to match *unharmed* with *not hurt; courageous* with *brave;* and *remarkable* with *amazing*.

Your turn

1   *... it was not only alive but also complete.*
What does the word *complete* tell you about the squid that was caught by the fisherman?   [1 mark]

_____

Read this

Daddy Fell into the Pond

Everyone grumbled. The sky was grey.
We had nothing to do and nothing to say.
We were nearing the end of a dismal day,
And there seemed to be nothing beyond,
　　　　THEN
　　　Daddy fell into the pond!
And everyone's face grew merry and bright,
And Timothy danced for sheer delight.
"Give me the camera, quick, oh quick!
He's crawling out of the duckweed."
　　　Click!

By Alfred Noyes

Top tip

If you are given two answer lines, give two different answers. Write one word on each answer line.

Let's try

What does the word *dismal* tell you about the day the family had had?

Tick **one**.

It was …

exciting	☐	miserable	☐
funny	☐	quiet	☐

1 Read the question and read it again. What do you have to do?

I need to choose a word from the list that can mean *dismal*.

2 What do you know about the family's day?

It wasn't good. They were grumbling. They had nothing to do.

3 Try each word in the list in place of the word *dismal*.

I need to check the sentence each time.

4 Choose the one that is closest in meaning. Your word should not change the meaning of the sentence. Check your answer.

The word that fits best is *miserable*. ☑

Your turn

1 … *Timothy danced for sheer delight.*

Timothy was happy. **Find** and **copy two** words that show the rest of the family were feeling happy too.

[2 marks]

1 _____   2 _____

Read this

Plop the Owl

So Plop shut his eyes, took a deep breath and fell off his branch. He floated down on his little white wings and landed like a feather.

Feeling very pleased with himself, he looked around. There were two strange lamps shining from the shadows under the tree. Plop went closer, and found that the lamps were a pair of un-winking eyes, and they belonged to a big black cat.

Plop waited for a minute, but what he was expecting to happen didn't.

From *The Owl Who Was Afraid of the Dark*
by Jill Tomlinson

Top tips

• If you are asked to **find** and **copy**, check whether you need to copy a *word*, a *group of words* or a *sentence*.

• Don't add any extra words. It might help to underline the word or words first.

Let's try

Find and copy a group of words that show Plop touched the ground very gently.

_____

1 Read the question and read it again. What do you have to do? | I need to find and copy a group of words that show Plop touched the ground gently.

2 Read the whole story again. Can you find any words that show this? | It says he *landed like a feather*. A feather is not heavy and would land gently.

3 Copy these words onto the answer line. Don't write any other words. | I need to write *landed like a feather*.

4 Check your answer.

Your turn

1 ... *two strange lamps shining from the shadows* ...

What do these words describe?   [1 mark]
Tick **one**.

the branches of the tree ☐   Plop's little wings ☐

the cat's eyes ☐   the streetlights ☐

The order of events

You need to show that you understand the **sequence** of **events**. This means explaining in what order things happen in different **texts** (pieces of writing).

Read this

Making Pancakes

We got out a big dish and I climbed on a stool and reached the flour down from the cupboard, knocking over the sugar as I did it. That was the first accident. You know what sugar's like – it seems to get all over the place – in the bread and butter, all over the floor, and some of it was on Ruthie's head. She didn't mind. She was licking it up as it trickled down her face. We put some of the flour in the dish and scraped the sugar into it off the table.

From *Making Pancakes When My Mother Was Out* by Paddy Kinsale

Top tips

- When you are asked to *Number the sentences,* write a different number in each box.
- Check your answer to see if the sentences are in the correct order.

Let's try

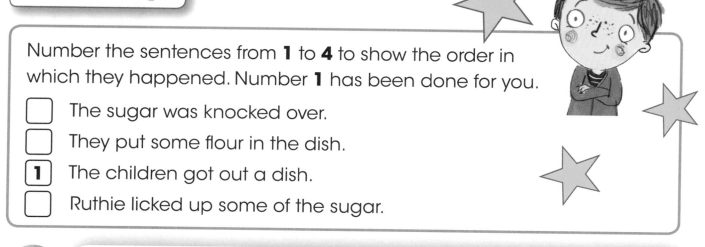

Number the sentences from **1** to **4** to show the order in which they happened. Number **1** has been done for you.

- ☐ The sugar was knocked over.
- ☐ They put some flour in the dish.
- ☑ 1 The children got out a dish.
- ☐ Ruthie licked up some of the sugar.

1 Read the question and read it again. What do you have to do?

I need to put the sentences in the right order.

2 What should you do first?

Read the story again. Find each event that is in the question.

3 Number 1 is done for you. Decide which sentence will be number 2. Then move on to number 3 and number 4. Check your answer.

The sentences should be numbered 2, 4, 1, 3.

Your turn

1 What was the **last** thing the children did?   [1 mark]

Tick **one**.

They put the sugar into the dish.   ☐

They got the flour from the cupboard.   ☐

They put sugar in Ruthie's hair.   ☐

They put the flour on the table.   ☐

Read this

Eating Food

Your food's journey starts when you put it into your mouth. Teeth crush your food so it's mushy enough to swallow. When you swallow, the food goes down a tube to your stomach. Food is squeezed and mushed up a lot in here. Juices are added here to mush up your food even more.

Your food travels through long, coiled-up tubes called intestines. It goes through the small intestine first ... then into the large intestine. Muscles in both tubes push the food along. Solid stuff is pushed out.

From *Look Inside Your Body* by Louie Stowell

Top tips

- Sometimes, there is more than one correct answer.
- Look carefully to see how many things the question asks for.

Let's try

Fill in the chart. Write **one** thing that happens.

1. You put food into your mouth.

2. _____

3. Food is squeezed and mushed up in your stomach.

1 Read the question and read it again. What do you have to do?

I need to write one thing that happens after you put food into your mouth and before the food is mushed up.

2 Read the text again.

I need to find the information in sentences **1** and **3**.

3 Now find one thing that happens in between these sentences.

Teeth crush your food. You swallow your food. Food goes down a tube into your stomach.

4 All these answers are correct. Choose one and write it next to the number **2**. Check your answer.

Your teeth crush your food.

Your turn

1 What happens **just before** your food goes through the large intestine?

[1 mark]

_____

35

Read this

Kitty and the Vegetables

"I don't want to eat my yukky veggy-troubles," shouted Kitty.

Instead of getting cross, Mum tried to persuade her. "Cabbage, carrots, green beans and cauliflower are good for you. They make you big and strong," she said.

"*You'll* never be bi-ig; *you'll* always be litt-le," sang Dan.

Kitty started to cry. She jumped down from the table and ran outside. She looked around the garden, and thought. Grass. **Nasturtium** leaves. All green. She took her toy wheelbarrow, and filled it with handfuls of grass and nasturtium leaves, and stirred it all round with a stick.

Glossary

nasturtium   a plant with
             round leaves

From *I Don't Want To!* by Bel Mooney

Top tips

- When you are given a list of choices, think about all the choices before ticking one.
- When you are asked to *Number the sentences,* keep checking your answer with the text.

Let's try

What did Kitty do **after** she ran outside?

Tick **one**.

jumped down from the table ☐   started to cry ☐

shouted at Mum ☐   got her wheelbarrow ☐

1 Read the question and read it again. What do you have to do? | I need to decide what Kitty did after she ran outside.

2 Find in the story where Kitty runs outside. What does she do **after** this? | She looks round the garden. She gets her wheelbarrow and fills it with grass.

3 Read all the answer choices. Which one fits best with what you have found? | got her wheelbarrow ☑

4 Check your answer.

Your turn

1 Number the sentences from **1** to **4** to show the order in which they happened. Number **1** has been done for you. [1 mark]

☐ Mum said vegetables would make Kitty strong.

[1] Kitty didn't want to eat her vegetables.

☐ Kitty started to cry.

☐ Dan teased Kitty.

Finding information

You need to show that you can use non-fiction **texts** to find key information.

Read this

Broad Bean Snack

Ask an adult to help you with this activity.

You will need:

vegetable oil

a handful of fresh broad beans taken out of their pods

salt

1. Ask an adult to heat the vegetable oil in a pan.
2. Add the broad beans to the hot oil and fry for three minutes, or until they are golden brown.
3. Remove the fried beans and drain them on kitchen paper.
4. Sprinkle a little salt over the beans, then serve.

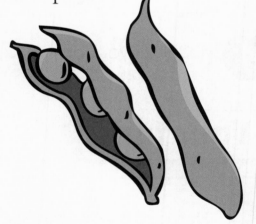

From *Grow Your Own Snack* by John Malam

Top tip

If you can't find the answer straight away, read the whole text again.

38

Let's try

When should you stop frying the beans?

Tick **one**.

when the vegetable oil is hot ☐

when they are out of their pods ☐

when they are golden brown ☐

when they are on kitchen paper ☐

1 Read the question and read it again. What do you have to do? | I need to say when you should stop frying the beans.

2 Read the text again. Which part is about frying the beans? | Step 2. It says fry them for three minutes or until they are golden brown.

3 Read all the answer choices. Which one fits best with what you have found? | when they are golden brown ✓

4 Check your answer.

Your turn

1 One of the things you need for this activity is salt. What is the salt used for?

[1 mark]

_____

Read this

Contents

What is happiness? 4

How does it feel to be happy? 6

What makes people happy? 8

What can I do to feel happy? 10

What if I am feeling sad? 12

How can I turn sad feelings into happy ones? 14

How can I make other people feel happy? 16

Make a happiness toolbox 18

From *Dealing with Feeling Happy* by Isabel Thomas

Top tip

If you are asked to *Draw a line to match,* only draw one line to each choice.

40

Let's try

Draw a line to match what you can read about with the page number.

what it feels like to be happy • •12

making other people feel happy • • 6

what to do if you feel sad • •16

1 Read the question and read it again. What do you have to do?

I need to match each thing with the page number from the contents page.

2 Find each of the things in the list of contents.

What it feels like to be happy is on page 6; *making other people happy* is on page 16.

3 Draw lines to match the first two. Can you find *what to do if you feel sad*? Check your answer.

This could be page 12 or page 14, but only 12 is left in the question. I need to draw my last line to 12.

Your turn

1 Which of the following can you read about in this book? [1 mark]

Tick **one**.

How to stop yourself feeling angry. ☐

How to make other people feel sad. ☐

How to make yourself feel happy. ☐

How it feels to help other people. ☐

Read this

Mountains

Mountains are high, rocky places. Their highest points are called peaks.

Snowy peaks

The higher up a mountain you go, the colder and windier it gets. On the high slopes, it is too cold for trees to grow.

Climbing creatures

Many mountain animals, such as goats and snow leopards, are excellent climbers.

Mighty mountains

A line of mountains is called a range. The Andes, in South America, is the longest mountain range in the world.

From *The Usborne Children's Picture Atlas* by Linda Edwards

Did you know?

In the mountains, you might see a:
- bald eagle
- yak
- Ural owl.

Top tip

Always check how many boxes you must tick.

Let's try

What does each section of the text tell you about?
Tick **one** box in each line.

One has been done for you.

	Animals in the mountains	Weather in the mountains
Climbing creatures	✓	
Snowy peaks		
Did you know?		

1 Read the question and read it again. What do you have to do?

I need to tick a box to say what each section of the text is about.

2 The first line has been done for you. Look at the second line in the table. What is *Snowy peaks* about?

It is about the weather. I need to tick *Weather in the mountains.*

3 Now look at the last line. What is *Did you know?* about? Check your answer.

It is about animals. I need to tick *Animals in the mountains.*

Your turn

1 The writer wants to add this new sentence to the text above.

They have extra-thick fur to keep out the wind.

Which section would the sentence best fit into? [1 mark]

_____

Read this

What's in Space?

Ever since people have lived on Earth, they've gazed at the sky and wondered what was up there.

4000 years ago

People saw shapes in the stars and made drawings of them. Stars grouped together in shapes are known as constellations.

1608

The first telescope was designed by a Dutch **spectacles** maker.

1675

King Charles II built the Greenwich **Observatory** to help sailors **navigate** by using the stars.

1969

The first men landed on the moon.

From *See Inside Space* by Katie Daynes

Glossary

navigate	find the way
observatory	a building that has telescopes for looking at the stars
spectacles	glasses

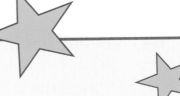

Top tips

In a table:
- read each part carefully
- tick only one of the boxes in each line.

Let's try

Put ticks in the table to show which sentences are **true** and which are **false**.
One has been done for you.

	True	False
King Charles II designed the first telescope.		
Groups of stars are known as constellations.	✓	
The Greenwich Observatory was built in 1969.		

1 Read the question and read it again. What do you have to do?

I need to tick to show whether each sentence is true or false.

2 Read the information again. Look at the first sentence in the table. Does it match the text?

No. The text says that a Dutch spectacles maker designed the first telescope. I need to tick *False* in the first line.

3 The next line has been done for you. Now look at the last line about the Observatory. Check your answer.

This sentence is not true. It was built in 1675. I need to tick *False* in the last line.

Your turn

1 How did King Charles II help sailors? [1 mark]
Tick **one**.
He helped them to:

make drawings of the stars ☐   land on the moon ☐
find their way using the stars ☐   make spectacles ☐

Character and events

You need to understand the **characters** and **events** (things that happen) in different kinds of **text** (e.g. in a story or poem). You may need to find important details or use your understanding of the whole text.

Read this

George and Grandpa

George was keen to get on and save the world. He quickly ate his breakfast and tossed his **leftovers** in the bin. "Slow down, George," said Grandpa. "We might be able to use some of that again."

"But it's rubbish," said George, looking puzzled.

"Aha," laughed Grandpa, "don't be too sure."

"Now turn that light off, Superboy," said Grandpa, "and then we'll hang out the washing."

"I don't have time to hang out washing," said George. "I'm a world-saving superhero, you know!"

"EXACTLY" said Grandpa. "Saving electricity will help you save the world."

Glossary
leftovers   food that has not been eaten

From *George Saves the World by Lunchtime* by Jo Readman

Top tips

- If you can't find the answer straight away, read the text again, more closely.
- Always read to the end of the text.

Let's try

Why does Grandpa tell George to turn the light off?

_____

1 Read the question and read it again. What do you have to do?

I need to say why Grandpa tells George to turn off the light.

2 Find this part of the story. Can you find Grandpa's reason for saying this?

I can find what he says but can't find his reason.

3 Read on to the end of the story. The answer might be further on in the text.

I've found the answer. He tells George to turn the light off to save electricity.

4 Check your answer.

Your turn

1 What does George want to save? [1 mark]

_____

2 Grandpa doesn't want George to throw his leftovers in the bin.

Find and **copy** the word that George uses to describe his leftovers. [1 mark]

_____

Read this

The Swing

How do you like to go up in a swing,
Up in the air so blue?
Oh, I do think it the pleasantest thing
Ever a child can do!

Up in the air and over the wall,
Till I can see so wide,
Rivers and trees and cattle and all
Over the countryside –

Till I look down on the garden green,
Down on the roof so brown –
Up in the air I go flying again,
Up in the air and down!

By Robert Louis Stevenson

Top tips

If you are asked to **find** and **copy**:
• check whether the question asks you to copy a *word* or a *line*
• copy exactly from the text. It will help to underline the word
  or words first.

Let's try

Find and copy one line that tells you the poet can see for a long way.

_____

1 Read the question and read it again. What do you have to do?

I need to find and copy one line in the poem that shows the poet can see a long way.

2 Read the whole poem again. Can you find any lines that show this?

Till I can see so wide gives the idea of seeing a long way. So does *Over the countryside.*

3 Choose **one** of these lines and copy it onto the answer line. Do not write any other words.

I will write *Till I can see so wide.*

4 Check your answer.

Your turn

1 What does the poet like about being on a swing?   [1 mark]
Tick **one**.

being with other children ☐   feeling like he is flying ☐

coming down to the ground ☐   landing on the wall ☐

Read this

Harry and the Dinosaurs

The sound that the plastic dinosaurs made as they rattled softly on to the dusty planks gave him a start. Even though it had been years since he'd played with his bucketful of dinosaurs, it felt like it was only yesterday. There was something about the way the little **triceratops**' legs slid between his fingers and the familiar prickle of its horns against the tip of his thumb that made him smile. He put the triceratops down carefully and picked up the winged **lizard**. "You should be a **pteranodon**, not a **pterodactyl**," he muttered to himself. "And you're not even a dinosaur really."

Suddenly he felt silly. He was *way* too old for games with toy dinosaurs and here he was talking to them again!

From *Harry and the Dinosaurs: The Flying Save* by Ian Whybrow

Glossary	
lizard	an animal with skin like a snake and four legs; a reptile
triceratops, pteranodon, pterodactyl	kinds of dinosaur

Top tip

Think about all the choices in the list before ticking one.

50

Let's try

When did Harry last play with his dinosaurs?

_____

1 Read the question and read it again. What do you have to do? | I need to say when Harry last played with his dinosaurs.

2 Read the story again. What does it say about this? | It says it had been years since he'd played with them.

3 What does this mean? | It means it was a long time ago.

4 Write your answer. Check your answer. | Harry last played with his dinosaurs a long time ago.

Your turn

1 At the end, why did Harry feel silly? [1 mark]

Tick **one**.

He couldn't remember the dinosaurs' names. ☐

He thought he was too old to play with dinosaurs. ☐

He jumped when the dinosaurs made a rattling noise. ☐

He pricked his thumb on one of the dinosaur's horns. ☐

Read this

Space Poem

The sun is like
a gold balloon

the moon
a silver pearl

the earth is like
a marble blue

the milky way
a creamy swirl.

If stars are like
those little boats

afloat a sea
of night

the dark is when
a hand comes down

and switches
off the light!

By James Carter

Top tip

When you are asked to *Draw a line to match,* only draw one line to each choice.

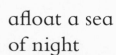

Let's try

What does the poem say the dark is like?
Tick **one**.

a blue marble ☐   the light going out ☐

a boat on the sea ☐   the milky way ☐

1 Read the question and read it again. What do you have to do?

I need to find what the poem says the dark is like.

2 Read the poem again. What does it say about the dark?

It says it is like when someone switches off the light.

3 Read all the answer choices. Which one fits best with what you have found? Check your answer.

the light going out ✓

Your turn

1 Draw a line to match each thing with what the poem says it is like.

[1 mark]

the sun •   • little boats

the moon •   • a gold balloon

the stars •   • a silver pearl

Explaining what you have read

You need to explain what happens in a **text** (piece of writing), what **characters** do, and the information you have read. You also need to understand the titles of different kinds of **text**. You may need to explain why a writer has chosen to use certain words in a title.

Read this

Mr Crocodile

"I've been thinking," Mrs Crocodile began as Mr Crocodile started on the dishes. "I'm sick and tired of living in this **dank**, dark, smelly hole in the riverbank."

"But this is how crocodiles live, dear!" Mr Crocodile exclaimed. "I thought we were happy!"

"Well, I am not. All you do is float around on your belly all day trying to look like a log so you can catch poor, helpless, harmless animals."

"But that's what crocodiles do, dear!" cried Mr Crocodile, all hurt and **in a huff**. "It's not as if we're **vegetarians**!"

"There must be something more useful you could do," Mrs Crocodile continued.

From *Mr Crookodile* by John Bush

Glossary

dank	wet and cold
in a huff	annoyed
vegetarian	someone who does not eat meat

Top tip

If the question asks *Why*, you need to explain your answer.

Let's try

How did Mrs Crocodile feel about where they were living? **Why**?

_____

_____

1 | Read the question and read it again. What do you have to do? | I need to say how Mrs Crocodile felt about where they lived and why. I need to explain my answer.

2 | What do you know about how Mrs Crocodile felt? | She was fed up. She didn't like it and was not happy.

3 | Can you find the reasons why she felt this way? | She thought their hole was wet, dark and smelly.

4 | Write **how** she felt and **why**. Check your answer. | Mrs Crocodile was not happy about where they lived because she thought it was wet, dark and smelly.

Your turn

1 Why might Mr Crocodile feel surprised at what Mrs Crocodile says?

Tick **one**.   [1 mark]

They are the same as other crocodiles. ☐

He is doing the washing up. ☐

He doesn't like the way they live. ☐

They float around all day. ☐

Read this

Hedgehogs are nocturnal, which means they only come out at night. During the day, hedgehogs will only sleep in a nest, so any hedgehog out during the day is probably in trouble or very poorly.

If you see a hedgehog out during the day, it will need to be picked up and taken to your nearest wildlife hospital as soon as possible. You can pick hedgehogs up using gardening gloves. You should put the hedgehog into a cardboard box, although they are good climbers when well, so you would need to make sure it cannot escape.

Adapted from St Tiggywinkles website

Top tip

If you are asked to think of a title, read the text again first. What is it about? Remember to explain why your title would be a good one.

Let's try

Why is it a problem if a hedgehog is out during the day?

_____

_____

1 Read the question and read it again. What do you have to do? | I need to decide why it is a problem if a hedgehog is out during the day.

2 Read the information again. Can you find any reasons why it is a problem? | Hedgehogs normally only come out at night. If they are out during the day they might be in trouble or poorly.

3 Write your answer. Make sure you explain why. | It is a problem because it means the hedgehog is probably poorly.

4 Check your answer.

Your turn

1 What title would you give this information text? [2 marks]

Title _____

Explain **why** you have chosen this title.

_____

Read this

The Adventure Holiday

I knew I'd hate it. I kept telling and telling
Dad. But he wouldn't listen to me.
He never does.
"I like the sound of this adventure holiday for children,"
said Dad, pointing to the advert in the paper. "**Abseiling**,
canoeing, **archery**, mountain biking ..."
"Sounds a bit dangerous to me," said Mum.
I didn't say anything. I went on watching telly.
"How about it, Tim?" said Dad. "What about
an adventure holiday, eh?"
"You can't be serious! Tim's much too
young," said Mum.
I still didn't say anything. I went on
watching telly. But my heart had
started thumping under my T-shirt.

From *Cliffhanger* by Jacqueline Wilson

Glossary	
abseiling	going down a steep cliff by sliding down a rope
archery	shooting with a bow and arrows

Top tip

When you are asked to say what you think, more than one answer can
be correct. The important thing is that you explain your choice.

Let's try

Do you think Tim is excited about the idea of an adventure holiday?

Tick **one**.

yes ☐   no ☐   yes and no ☐

Explain why you think this.

_____

_____

1 Read the question and read it again. What do you have to do?

I need to say whether Tim was excited about the idea of the holiday.

2 First you need to tick one box: *yes*, *no* or *yes and no*.

I think *no*, he wasn't excited.

3 Now explain why you think this. Check your answer.

He said he knew he would hate it. He watched TV instead of saying anything. His heart started thumping – this means he was scared.

Your turn

1 What does Mum think about the adventure holiday?   [1 mark]

_____

_____

Read this

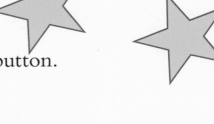

Oggy!

Oggy was a robot.
He had planned to go
travelling to **Jupiter**
in his **U-F-O**.

He packed his this.
He packed his that.
His blue guitar.
His purple cat.

It took a while
to pack it all –
his map, his hat,
his bat, his ball,

his bed, his boat,
his book, his broom.
His kitchen sink?
There wasn't room.

He locked the door.
He hummed awhile.
His radars bleeped.
He smiled a smile.

By James Carter

He pushed the button.
Time to go!
Engine started,
revved and ohhh …

It spluttered, made
a dreadful sound.
If lifted up then
crashed right down.

What was wrong?
His U-F-O
when stuffed with stuff
it would not go.

Oggy sighed.
He scratched his head.
He'd had enough.
And so, instead

he put his stuff
back in his shed.
And in a huff
he went to bed!

Glossary
Jupiter   a planet
U-F-O   a spaceship

Top tip

Think about all the choices in the list before ticking one.

Let's try

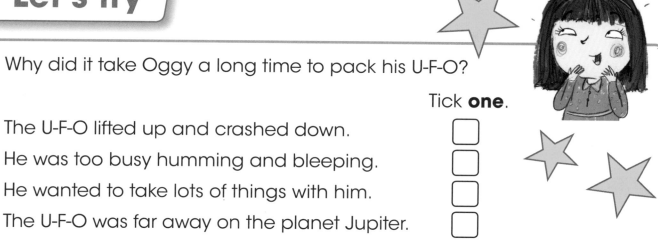

Why did it take Oggy a long time to pack his U-F-O?

Tick **one**.

The U-F-O lifted up and crashed down. ☐

He was too busy humming and bleeping. ☐

He wanted to take lots of things with him. ☐

The U-F-O was far away on the planet Jupiter. ☐

1 Read the question and read it again. What do you have to do?

I need to decide why it took Oggy a long time to pack.

2 Read the poem again. Can you find any reasons why?

He is packing lots of things, like his bed and his boat.

3 Read all the answer choices. Which one fits best with what you have found? Check your answer.

He wanted to take lots of things with him. ✓

Your turn

1 What would be another good title for the poem? [2 marks]

Title _____

Explain **why** you have chosen this title.

_____

Glossary

character	a person (or animal) in a story
event	something that happens
phrase	a group of words that make sense, e.g. *a red rose*
predict	say what will or might happen
sequence	order
text	a piece of writing, e.g. a story, a poem, a set of instructions

Answers

Page 9   Making inferences (1d)
1. He is too excited to sleep. ✓

Page 11   Making inferences (1d)
1. (*They are*) *easily scared*

Page 13   Making inferences (1d)
1. *excited* ✓
2. He threw some things on the floor. / He made a mess in his room.

Page 15   Making inferences (1d)
1. **One** mark for reference to the snowman melting/becoming a puddle.

Two marks for reference to the snowman melting/becoming a puddle because the house is hot/warm/has a fire.

Page 17   Making predictions (1e)
1. He might paint some food / some things to eat.

Page 19   Making predictions (1e)
1. "I thought they were ordinary beans!" ✓

Page 21   Making predictions (1e)
1. Plausible, text-based answers about what Mum might have said, e.g.:
   • *"Why did you do that?"*
   • *"You should have stayed in bed!"*
   • *"I am very cross with you, Kitty."*

Page 23   Vocabulary (1a)
1. *squirms*

Page 25   Vocabulary (1a)
1. Appropriate synonyms for *vast*, e.g. *big, enormous, huge*.

Page 27   Vocabulary (1a)
1. It was whole. / There was nothing missing.

Page 29   Vocabulary (1a)
1. **One** mark for each correct word, to a maximum of **two** marks:
   • *merry*
   • *bright*

NB: if the child writes "*merry and bright*" on just one answer line, award the maximum of **two** marks.

Page 31   Vocabulary (1a)
1. the cat's eyes ✓

Page 33   Sequencing (1c)
1. They put the sugar into the dish. ✓

Page 35   Sequencing (1c)
1. It goes through the small intestine.

Page 37   Sequencing (1c)
1. Mum said vegetables would make Kitty strong. 2
   Kitty didn't want to eat her vegetables. 1
   Kitty started to cry. 4
   Dan teased Kitty. 3

Page 39   Non-fiction texts (1b)
1. To sprinkle over the beans. / To finish them off before serving.

Page 41   Non-fiction texts (1b)
1. How to make yourself feel happy. ✓

Page 43   Non-fiction texts (1b)
1. *Climbing creatures* (or any unambiguous paraphrase of this section title, e.g. *Creatures*)
   Also accept: *Did you know?*

Page 45   Non-fiction texts (1b)
1. find their way using the stars ✓

ANSWERS

Page 47 Fiction and poetry (1b)

1. *the world*

2. *(it's) rubbish (said George)*

Page 49 Fiction and poetry (1b)

1. feeling like he is flying

Page 51 Fiction and poetry (1b)

1. He thought he was too old to play with dinosaurs. ✓

Page 53 Fiction and poetry (1b)

1. One mark for all correctly matched:

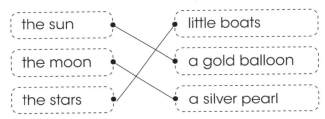

the sun	little boats
the moon	a gold balloon
the stars	a silver pearl

Page 55 Understand and explain (1b)

1. They are the same as other crocodiles. ✓

Page 57 Understand and explain (1b)

1. One mark for an appropriate text-based title, e.g. *Hedgehogs in trouble; Hedgehogs out in the day; How to help a poorly hedgehog.*

Two marks for an appropriate title and text-based explanation for this, e.g.:

- *Hedgehogs in trouble because it's about how hedgehogs who are out in the day need help.*
- *How to help a poorly hedgehog because it tells you how to pick it up and what to do with it.*

Page 59 Understand and explain (1b)

1. She thinks it sounds dangerous. / She thinks Tim is too young.

Page 61 Understand and explain (1b)

1. One mark for an appropriate text-based title, e.g. *The U-F-O; Oggy's Trip.*

Two marks for an appropriate title and text-based explanation for this, e.g.:

- *The U-F-O because Oggy packs his U-F-O full of stuff.*